796.756   Abdo, Kenny
ABD   Motorcross

ANNIE E VINTON ELEMENTARY

SCHOOL LIBRARY

306 STAFFORD ROAD

MANSFIELD CENTER, CT 06250

ACTION SPORTS

MOTOCROSS

KENNY ABDO

abdopublishing.com

Published by Abdo Zoom, a division of ABDO, P.O. Box 398166, Minneapolis, Minnesota 55439. Copyright © 2018 by Abdo Consulting Group, Inc. International copyrights reserved in all countries. No part of this book may be reproduced in any form without written permission from the publisher.

Printed in the United States of America, North Mankato, Minnesota.
092017
012018

THIS BOOK CONTAINS
RECYCLED MATERIALS

Photo Credits: iStock, Shutterstock
Production Contributors: Kenny Abdo, Jennie Forsberg, Grace Hansen
Design Contributors: Dorothy Toth, Neil Klinepier

Publisher's Cataloging-in-Publication Data

Names: Abdo, Kenny, author.
Title: Motocross / by Kenny Abdo.
Description: Minneapolis, Minnesota: Abdo Zoom, 2018. | Series: Action sports |
    Includes online resource and index.
Identifiers: LCCN 2017939265 | ISBN 9781532120930 (lib.bdg.) |
    ISBN 9781532122057 (ebook) | ISBN 9781532122613 (Read-to-Me ebook)
Subjects: LCSH: Motocross--Juvenile literature. | Motor Sports--Juvenile
literature. | Extreme Sports—
    Juvenile literature.
Classification: DDC 796.756--dc23
LC record available at https://lccn.loc.gov/2017939265

TABLE OF CONTENTS

MOTOCROSS

Motocross is an **off-road** motorcycle **race** that was invented in the United Kingdom.

Motocross began as a sport after World War II, competing on horse race tracks.

TYPES

Dirt bikes are used in motocross **racing** in North America, Europe and Asia.

The dirt bikes are lightweight, **off-road** motorcycles. They have special tires to handle rough ground in all types of weather.

Dirt bikes are used because of their easy movements and smaller **engines**.

Dirt bikes are illegal to use on streets and highways. They are only allowed on proper courses.

COMPETITION

There are many forms of Motocross competition, like **freestyle**, freeriding, and big air.

Freestyle focuses on performing **stunts** like backflips and 360s while using motocross bikes to jump.

19

Supercross off-road races are on man-made dirt **tracks** that include big jumps and obstacles. They are mostly held at professional baseball and football stadiums.

GLOSSARY

engine – a machine that changes power into motion.

freestyle – an extreme sport centered on stunt riding.

off-road – riding a vehicle on difficult roads or tracks, like sand, mud, or gravel.

race – a competition of speed.

stunts – an action showing a great skill.

supercross – a racing sport using high-performance motorcycles.

tracks – a course laid out for racing, usually made of dirt.

World War II – a war fought in Europe, Asia, and Africa from 1939 to 1945.

ONLINE RESOURCES

Booklinks
NONFICTION NETWORK
FREE! ONLINE NONFICTION RESOURCES

To learn more about motocross, please visit abdobooklinks.com. These links are routinely monitored and updated to provide the most current information available.

INDEX